THE MIRACLE OF EASTER

Adapted by
Etta G. Wilson

Illustrations by
Thomas Gianni

Publications International, Ltd.

The morning after Jesus died, a man named Joseph from Arimathea got permission to bury his body. With the help of others, Joseph laid Jesus' body in a new tomb that had been carved out of solid rock. Then they rolled a big stone across the opening of the tomb.

The next day, the religious leaders of the country remembered what Jesus had said: "After three days I will rise again." They decided to send some Roman guards to watch the tomb.

That Sunday, something very amazing happened at the tomb. An earthquake shook the ground, and an angel of God appeared. He rolled away the stone that closed the tomb and sat on it.

The angel looked as bright as lightning, and his clothes were white as snow. The Roman guards were very afraid. They trembled and fell down, as though they were dead.

Then Jesus walked out of the tomb. He had returned to life, as he said he would!

A little later, some women who had known Jesus came to his tomb. They were surprised to see that the great stone had been moved. Inside the tomb, they saw the angel.

The angel said, "Jesus is not here. He has risen just as he said he would. Quickly now, go tell his followers that Jesus is alive! You will see him in Galilee."

The women were so excited. They left the tomb in a great hurry and ran to tell the disciples.

Meanwhile, some of the soldiers guarding the tomb went back to the city. They told the religious leaders what had happened.

The leaders were very surprised. They talked with one another and made their plan. They collected a lot of money and promised it to the soldiers if they would tell a great lie.

The soldiers agreed. They took the money and told their captain, "Jesus' disciples came at night and stole his body while we were asleep."

While this was happening, the women ran straight to the disciples and excitedly told them about Jesus' tomb and the angel. Most of the disciples thought the women must have made a mistake. But Peter and John ran to the tomb. There, they saw the strips of cloth that had been wrapped around Jesus' body, but Jesus was not there. The tomb was empty!

Quickly, they returned to tell the other disciples.

That same day, two of Jesus' disciples were going to a village outside Jerusalem. They were talking about everything that had happened. As they talked, another man came along and walked with them. It was Jesus, but the men didn't recognize him. He asked what the two were talking about.

One of the disciples said, "You must be the only man in the city who doesn't know what has happened."

Then both of them explained what had happened to Jesus.

Then Jesus began to explain everything that the ancient prophets had said about him. But the disciples still did not recognize him.

When they came to the village, the disciples asked him to spend the night with them. While they were eating dinner, Jesus took a loaf of bread, blessed it, and gave it to them. At that moment, they knew he was Jesus. Then he disappeared.

The two hurried back to Jerusalem to tell the other disciples that they had seen Jesus.

Later that same night, most of Jesus' disciples were together in Jerusalem. Suddenly, Jesus was in the room with them.

One disciple, named Thomas, was not there to see Jesus that night. When the others told him Jesus was alive, he said that he would not believe it unless he saw for himself.

About a week later, the disciples were together again. This time Thomas was there. And again Jesus came to them. He said to Thomas, "Touch me. Stop doubting and believe!

Thomas answered, "My Lord, I believe in you!"

༻༺

A few weeks later, Jesus met the disciples on a hill in Galilee. There, he told them, "Go to people everywhere and make them my disciples. Teach them what I have taught you. And remember, I will always be with you."

Then Jesus raised his hands and blessed the disciples. As he was blessing them, he was taken up into heaven.

The disciples gave thanks to God for the wonderful things that had happened. Then they went out and began to teach people about Jesus anywhere they could.